AMERICA GOES TO WAR

WORLD WAR I

TIMELINES, FACTS, AND BATTLES

By Craig Boutland

Published in 2023 by The Rosen Publishing Group, Inc.
2544 Clinton Street, Buffalo, NY 14224

Editor: Lindsey Lowe
Children's Publisher: Anne O'Daly
Design Manager: Keith Davis
Picture Manager: Sophie Mortimer

Picture Credits:
Front Cover:Everett Collection/Shutterstock.com
Key: t = top, b = bottom, c = center
All Photographs The Robert Hunt Library except, Alamy: Historic Collection 40-45, 51b; Imperial War Museum: 11t, 16t, 60-61c; Library of Congress: 10-11b, 11b, 16-17b, 22t, 23t, 29b, 51t, 61t; National Portrait Gallery: 10b; Pubic Domain: 35t, 45c, 50-51c, 50-51b, 60-61b, Biblioteque Nationale de France/Agence Roi 34bl, David King Collection/Tate Gallery/Scala Archives 51t, Digital Library of Slovenia 34-35b, Diverse/Unbekannt 28b, gebirgskrieg.heim 35b, Gutenberg.org 28t, 29t, Krisalistadt 50-51b, La Dominica del Corriere/Achille Beltrame 34t, Max Smith/Megapixie 17t, New York World 60, Robert Sennecke 22b; United States Government: U.S. Airforce 44b, 44t, U.S. Navy/Naval Historical Center 10-11c, U.S. War Department 16c, USN/Naval Aviation News 45t.

Cataloging-in-Publication Data

Names: Boutland, Craig.
Title: World War I: timelines, facts, and battles / Craig Boutland.
Description: New York : Rosen Publishing, 2023. | Series: America goes to war| Includes bibliographic references, index and glossary.
Identifiers: ISBN 9781499473940 (pbk) | ISBN 9781499473957 (library bound) | ISBN 9781499473964 (ebook)
Subjects: LCSH: World War, 1914-1918- —Juvenile literature
Classification: LCC D521 B68 2023 | DDC 940.3—dc23

Manufactured in the United States of America

CPSIA Compliance Information: Batch #CWRYA23. For further information contact Rosen Publishing at 1-800-237-9932.

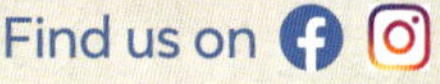

CONTENTS

Introduction

For those who lived through it, the conflict that engulfed much of the world from 1914 to 1918 was known as "The Great War" or "The War to End War."

World War I was fought on a previously unimaginable scale. More than 35 million people died. The image of hundreds of thousands of soldiers dying for little gain in the mud of the Western Front became a lasting symbol of the futility of war.

The Course of the War

The causes of the war lay in rivalries among Europe's great powers. The assassination of an Austrian archduke in 1914 triggered a chain reaction that rapidly brought millions into military service. The Germans raced to defeat their French neighbors before turning to face the Russians; the failure of their plan left them fighting on two fronts. In the west, the armies dug lines of trenches that would barely move for five years, despite enormous loss of life. Aircraft clashed in dogfights above the trenches, while zeppelin airships launched the first air raids on civilians. An attempt by the Allies (Britain and its empire, France, and Russia) to open a new front in Turkey failed at Gallipoli. At sea, warships clashed rarely, but one intervention—the sinking of the liner *Lusitania* by a German submarine—changed the course of the war by drawing in the United States. The arrival of U.S. forces would finally break the deadlock on the Western Front and open the way to Allied victory.

About This Book

This book contains two types of timelines. Along the bottom of the pages is a timeline that covers the whole period. It lists key events and developments, color coded to indicate the Western Front, Eastern Front, and other theaters of the war. Each chapter also has its own timeline, which runs vertically down the sides of the pages. This timeline gives more specific details about the particular subject of the chapter. IN FOCUS spreads give more information on battles, weapons, and personalities.

The crew of a British 12-inch (30 cm) howitzer prepares to open fire at the start of the Battle of Arras in April 1917.

Causes of the War

In 1914, many European leaders wanted their countries to be strong and rich. They were prepared to take from other countries and fight wars to achieve their aims.

➔ German troops head west at the opening of their great offensive against Belgium and France in August 1914.

TIMELINE **1914 JUNE-JULY**

KEY: Western Front | Eastern Front | Other Fronts

June

June 28 Bosnia
Archduke Franz Ferdinand and his wife assassinated by a Serb during their visit to Sarajevo.

Although it soon involved countries and people from virtually every continent on Earth, World War I began as a European conflict. The United States, the only major world power outside Europe, did not join the war until later, in 1917.

Powerful European Rivals

The map of Europe in 1914 was very different from that of today. There were five "great powers": Germany, Austria-Hungary, France, Russia, and Britain. They had formed two opposing alliances: Austria-Hungary and Germany (the Central Powers) on one side and on the other, Britain, France, and Russia, known as the Entente (or Allies). The powers were economic rivals; many were carving out overseas empires, and the majority had potentially huge armies supplied by enormous armament industries. Such factors caused great suspicion between the two power blocs. Their rivalries needed just one event to drag them into physical conflict.

KEY DATES

June 28, 1914 Franz Ferdinand, heir to the throne of the Austro-Hungarian Empire, is assassinated in Sarajevo, the capital of Bosnia, by a Serb.

July 25, 1914 Serbia rejects Austria-Hungary demands that Serbia become part of their empire; the Austrians prepare for war with Serbia, which Russia is committed to protect.

August 1, 1914 Germany, an ally of Austria-Hungary, declares war on Russia.

August 3, 1914 Germany declares war on France, an ally of Russia.

August 4, 1914 Great Britain and its empire declare war on the Central Powers.

A Bosnian official greets Archduke Franz Ferdinand shortly before his assassination.

July

July 23 Austria-Hungary The Austro-Hungarians issue an ultimatum to Serbia that would bring to an end Serbia's existence as an independent state.

July 25 Serbia Serbia rejects the Austro-Hungarian ultimatum; Russian Czar Nicholas II mobilizes troops ready to protect Serbia.

July 29 Germany Germany begins to mobilize its High Seas Fleet.

July 31 Germany Germany informs Russia that it must halt its mobilization.

Germany's War Plans

In 1914, the German army was the most powerful in Europe. Count Alfred von Schlieffen, a former chief of staff, had come up with the plan on which German strategy was based in 1914. It relied on railroads to move troops around rapidly. However, war can rarely be exactly planned or predicted. Events soon proved that Schlieffen's "war by timetable" was impossible.

The Schlieffen Plan

Germany's military leaders feared having a war on two fronts, simultaneously fighting the Russians and French. However, they believed that the Russians would take longer to mobilize their armies. Count Alfred von Schlieffen therefore devised a plan to be followed if war began: France was to be quickly defeated before the Germans turned to face Russia.

War Begins

In 1914, Austria-Hungary, Germany, and Russia became involved in a quarrel over Serbia, a small country friendly to Russia. After a member of Austria-Hungary's royal family, Archduke Franz Ferdinand, was assassinated by a Serb, Austria-Hungary used the event as an excuse to declare war on Serbia on July 28. The system of alliances then kicked in; one by one, members of the rival alliances declared war on each other.

→ Count Alfred von Schlieffen planned Germany's strategy of attacking France.

TIMELINE **1914 AUGUST**

KEY: Western Front | Eastern Front | Other Fronts

August

August 1 Germany
Germany formally declares war on Russia.

August 3 Germany
Germany declares war on Russia's ally, France.

August 4 Britain
Britain formally declares war on Germany.

August 4 United States
The United States declares itself neutral.

August 5 Belgium
Germany fails to take Liege, a key border defense and railroad center.

August 7 France
The first troops of Britain's Expeditionary Force (BEF) arrive in France.

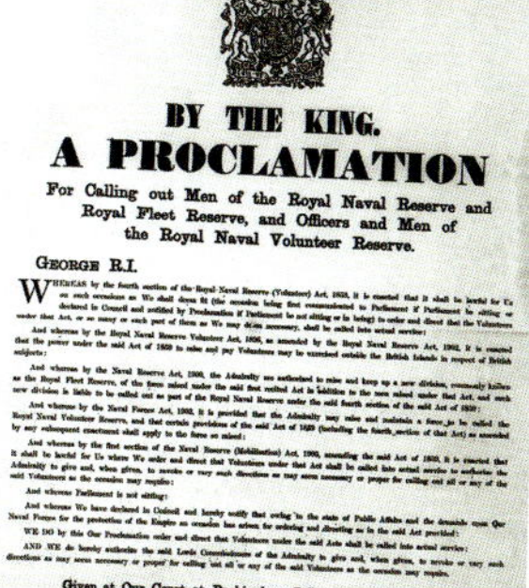
BY THE KING.

A PROCLAMATION

For Calling out Men of the Royal Naval Reserve and Royal Fleet Reserve, and Officers and Men of the Royal Naval Volunteer Reserve.

GEORGE R.I.

Given at Our Court at Buckingham Palace, this Third day of August, in the year of our Lord one thousand nine hundred and fourteen, and in the Fifth year of Our Reign.

GOD SAVE THE KING.

→ The British government's mobilization order was published in 1914.

Germany's Motives

Germany was eager to capture valuable coalfields along either side of the French and Belgian border. More importantly, the Schlieffen Plan called for the full-scale invasion and defeat of France before the German armies traveled east to fight the Russians. As soon as war was declared, therefore, events became inevitable. A race began to mobilize fighting forces and get them into the field. According to contemporary military theory, even a day's delay could mean the difference between ultimate victory and defeat.

Mobilization

Peacetime armies were generally far smaller than those in wartime. To get to full strength, armies had to mobilize their troops. They had to summon reservists (who had military training) from civilian life, equip them, and get them to the war zone. Because millions of people were involved, the process took time. No one wanted to let their opponents gain an advantage, so once one country started mobilizing, everyone else did the same.

← Germany gave the light cruiser *Breslau* to its Turkish allies as a gift.

August 12 Serbia
Austro-Hungarian troops forced to withdraw after five days of fighting.

August 14 France
First clash of Battle of the Frontiers between France and Germany.

August 16 Belgium
Liege falls to the Germans.

August 23 Belgium
The BEF drives the Germans back in another clash of the Battle of the Frontiers.

August 26 East Prussia
The Germans defeat the Russian Second Army at Tannenberg to end the Russian invasion of East Prussia.

August 28 North Sea
The British gain the upper hand over the German navy in the Battle of Heligoland Bight.

The Naval Arms Race

In the decade before 1914, the British and Germans began a race to create the most modern navy in the world.

One of the major reasons for international tensions before 1914 was what was called the Naval Arms Race. During the 19th century, Britain had controlled the world's sea lanes through the enormous number of warships of the Royal Navy. Late in the century, however, technological advances meant that a new generation of ships came into being. German admiral Alfred von Tirpitz saw an opportunity to catch up with Britain's naval might and Germany began building new battleships. Britain, under its head of the Royal Navy, "Jackie" Fisher, responded by accelerating a building program for new battleships known as Dreadnoughts.

Jutland

The two navies eventually clashed at the Battle of Jutland in 1916. Germany's ships proved technologically superior, but the Royal Navy won a key strategic victory. The German fleet did not challenge the Royal Navy again.

4

5

KEY DATES

November 1859 The first steam-powered ironclad warship, the French *La Gloire*, is launched. Before this, warships had been driven by sail alone and had hulls made of wood.

March 9, 1862 Battle of the Hampton Roads during the U.S. Civil War. The first clash between ironclad warships.

1892 Alfred von Tirpitz becomes head of the German navy. He oversees a naval building program to create a navy to take on Britain's fleet. In 1914, the German High Seas Fleet is approximately 40 percent the size of the Royal Navy, and includes 17 battleships.

February 1906 The Royal Navy battleship *Dreadnought* is launched. This is a revolution in naval design. It mounts ten 12-inch (30 cm) guns and has 11 inches (28 cm) of armor at its thickest point.

May 31, 1916 Battle of Jutland begins. The Royal Navy loses three capital ships and the Germans just one, but the German fleet thereafter remains in harbor.

1 HMS *Dreadnought* puts to sea in 1906. It revolutionized the design of capital ships, marking a new stage in the naval arms race.

2 John Arbuthnot Fisher, always known as "Jackie," was determined to keep the Royal Navy ahead of the Germans in naval building.

3 The 12-inch guns of *Dreadnought* made it more powerful than any other warship afloat on its launch in 1906.

4 HMS *Queen Mary* meets its end at the Battle of Jutland in 1916. The battle cruiser was one of three British capital ships lost.

5 John Jellicoe, admiral of the fleet. He held an awesome responsibility. It was said that he was the only man who could lose the war in an afternoon.

The Outbreak of War

The Western Front was the war's major military theater. The most important parts of the French and German armies fought from the North Sea to Switzerland.

→ A German howitzer could lob a large shell accurately up to 10,000 yards (9,140 m).

TIMELINE 1914 SEPTEMBER-OCTOBER

KEY: Western Front | Eastern Front | Other Fronts

September

September 5 France
French and British counterattack in the Battle of the Marne.

September 9 France
The Germans suffer their first defeat as they withdraw from near Paris in the Battle of the Marne.

September 9 East Prussia
German victory in the Battle of the Masurian Lakes sees heavy Russian losses.

September 15-18 France
The Battle of the Aisne. The British and French try to outmaneuver the Germans with little success in the Race to the Sea.

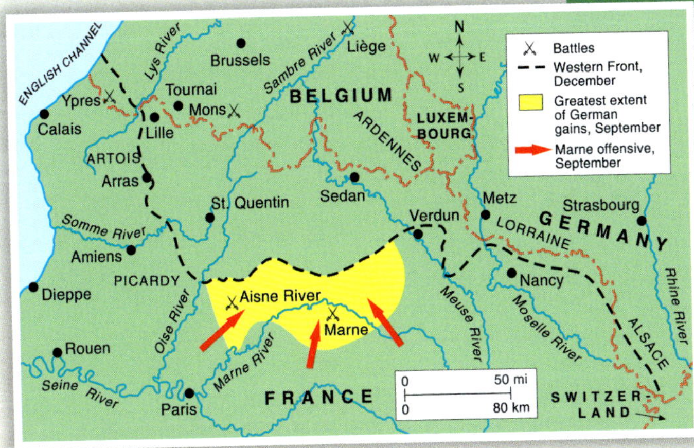

When war broke out in 1914, France saw a chance to get revenge for its defeat by the Germans in the Franco-Prussian War (1870–1871) and to recover territory it had subsequently lost to Germany on its eastern border. France had called up about 1.3 million troops in five armies. Its strategy was for three armies to launch all-out attacks in order to recapture the lost territory.

France's commander in chief, General Joseph Joffre, realized that the Germans might try to outflank his forces by invading France from farther north, through Belgium. He held back his other two armies to guard against that possibility. While Joffre's suspicion was correct, he underestimated the size of the potential

The German generals believed that they could conquer France in a matter of weeks in 1914.

KEY DATES

August 3, 1914 Germany invades Belgium.

August 4, 1914 Germany rejects Britain's demand that its troops leave Belgium. The British declare war on Germany at 11:00 p.m.

August 4, 1914 The United States declares itself neutral.

August 16, 1914 After days of German shelling, the Belgian city of Liege surrenders.

August 20, 1914 The Germans capture the Belgian capital, Brussels.

August 23, 1914 At Mons, the British push back a German attack but then retreat; the clash marks the end of the Battle of the Frontiers.

August 30, 1914 Paris is bombed by the Germans.

Continued on page 15

October

October 18–28 France/Belgium The Germans fail to capture key channel ports; the BEF clashes with the Germans at the First Battle of Ypres.

October 23 Mesopotamia British forces land in southern Mesopotamia and force the Turkish forces there to retreat.

October 29 Turkey The Turks declare war on the side of the Central Powers and shell Russian ports on the Black Sea.

October 29–November 24 Belgium The French and British stop the German advance at Ypres. Both sides start digging in, creating long lines of trenches.

German attack through Belgium. The Germans swept rapidly through Belgium, ignoring its request to remain neutral. As Britain had guaranteed Belgian independence, it now found itself with no option but to declare war on Germany and enter the war.

The German success in Belgium forced Allied forces to pull back south into France. By the start of September, the Allies had retreated almost as far as Paris, but a gap had opened in the German front. Backed by new reserve forces, the French and British targeted this vulnerable gap at the Battle of the Marne. The Allied victory there forced the Germans to retreat. Germany's gamble on the Schlieffen Plan had failed. There would be no quick victory over France.

Christmas 1914

On Christmas Day 1914, at a number of places on the Western Front, the bitter enemies of the previous summer and fall climbed out of their trenches under flags of truce. In "no-man's land," they chatted and exchanged gifts of tobacco, alcohol, and chocolate. The military authorities feared that such "fraternization" might make soldiers less willing to fight. They made sure that the truce was not repeated on other Christmas Days during the conflict.

→ British infantry take cover by a French roadside during the "Race to the Sea."

TIMELINE **1914 NOVEMBER-DECEMBER**

KEY: Western Front | Eastern Front | Other Fronts

November

November 1 Pacific
A German naval squadron damages a British squadron off Coronel, in Chile.

November 5-30 Serbia
Austro-Hungarian troops launch an advance toward Belgrade, which falls on December 2.

November 11-25 Eastern Front
After coming close to defeat by the German Ninth Army at Lódz, Russian forces counterattack and drive the enemy back.

Race to the Sea

The two sets of armies were now in eastern France, north of Paris. From late September until November, each side tried to outflank the other to the north in the so-called Race to the Sea. A series of vicious but indecisive battles brought the armies closer to the English Channel, ending in the southern Belgium city of Ypres. Neither side was able to find an open flank to attack the enemy.

Digging In

Both armies were exhausted and short of supplies; all countries had expected a short war. As generals retired to their headquarters to plan for the spring of 1915, the soldiers were left to defend their front lines through the winter. They began to dig trenches that soon spread along the length of the Western Front.

Continued from page 13

September 5, 1914 The Battle of the Marne sees French and British forces counterattack along the Marne River between Paris and Verdun.

September 9, 1914 After a decisive defeat, the Germans withdraw from near Paris, marking the end of the Battle of the Marne.

September 15–18, 1914 In the Battle of the Aisne, both sides try to outflank each other as part of the Race to the Sea.

October 29–November 24, 1914 The First Battle of Ypres. Germany fails to break through the Allied front; both sides dig trenches that will soon stretch from the North Sea down to the Swiss border.

December 25, 1914 The Christmas truce: German and British soldiers meet in "no-man's land."

British and German troops meet during an unauthorized truce on Christmas Day 1914.

December

December 8 South Atlantic Ocean
British warships surprise German ships off Argentina, sinking four, including *Scharnhorst* and *Gneisenau*.

December 14 France/Belgium
British and French offensives along the Western Front end in stalemate. The First Battle of Champagne continues through the winter.

December 18 Britain
The British declare a protectorate over Egypt and move troops to protect the strategically important Suez Canal.

The Machine Gun

The deadly rattle of the machine gun changed warfare forever in 1914.

Automatic weapons had been developed as early as the 1860s, but it was in the 1880s that Hiram Maxim invented his "Maxim Gun." This could fire bullets at a rate of 600 per second. The problem of overheating was solved by a jacket filled with water surrounding the barrel. Such weapons proved effective when used by western colonial forces in warfare in Africa. They were also used during the Russo-Japanese War (1904-1905.) Companies in other countries, such as Vickers in Britain and Hotchkiss in France, developed similar weapons.

Cover in the Trenches

In 1914, machine guns were used to devastating effect against groups of infantry or cavalry attacking over open country. Combined with rolls of barbed wire that slowed movement, machine guns made it almost impossible for attackers to dislodge dug-in defenders. Machine guns were set to fire on fixed lines, so that they were accurate and a synchronized group of them could make it impossible for infantry to cross a stretch of ground without incurring unacceptably high casualties. On the Western Front, infantry lived in trenches, barely daring to venture out.

1

2

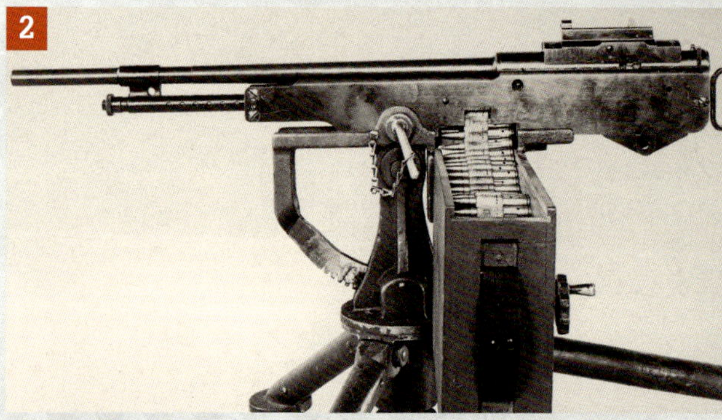

3

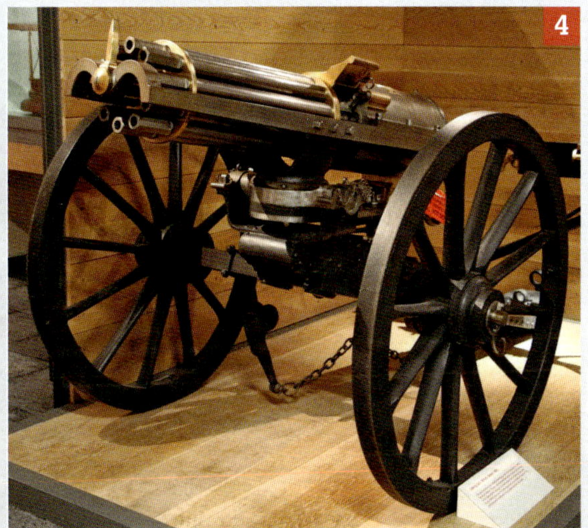

KEY DATES

1861 A patent is taken out for the Gatling gun, the first effective automatic weapons system. Gatling guns are used to a limited extent in the Civil War. They stand high off the ground, making their crews vulnerable to artillery fire and snipers.

1896 Vickers buys the Maxim Company, which has been producing machine guns since 1884, and creates its own machine gun with a .303 inch calibre.

1912 U.S. Army infantry regiments are issued four machine guns each. By 1918, toward the end of the war, 336 machine guns were issued to each infantry regiment.

1918 Because of production problems with the Browning M1917, the U.S. Expeditionary Force in France mainly uses French-made Hotchkiss machine guns.

March, 1918 German storm troopers attack Allied positions equipped with portable automatic weapons, such as the MP 18, called submachine guns.

1 A Vickers machine gun, the standard British army machine gun by the end of the war. The photo may be of a Scots regiment.

2 A .30 calibre machine gun. The number of machine guns per regiment increased enormously in the U.S. Army during the war.

3 U.S. soldiers in training with a Lewis gun. This automatic weapon featured a circular drum magazine on top of the breech.

4 An 1865 Gatling gun clearly showing the multiple barrels that permitted it to deliver automatic fire.

5 A German storm trooper armed with an MP 18 submachine gun. Storm troopers were trained to take enemy trenches and then move on.

The Eastern Front

The war on the Eastern Front began badly for Germany and Austria-Hungary, but the two powers recovered quickly and began to launch new attacks.

Some of the 90,000 Russian prisoners captured during the Battle of Tannenberg wait in line for rations.

TIMELINE 1915 JANUARY–MARCH

KEY: Western Front | Eastern Front | Other Fronts

January

January 13 Britain
Naval attack on the Dardanelles channel in Turkey is planned by the western Allies.

January 19–20 Britain
German zeppelin airships bomb eastern England, but do the minimum of damage.

January 24 North Sea
British warships successfully attack German ships in the Battle of the Dogger Bank.

February

February 1 Germany
The German government decides to allow its U-boats (submarines) to sink ships, even neutral vessels, without warning.

Facing Serbia to the south and Russia to the east, Austria-Hungary's chief of staff, General Franz Conrad von Hötzendorf, could not decide which front should have priority. The result was defeat in both sectors in 1914. Outnumbered Serbs fought the Austro-Hungarians to a standstill in August and September 1914, while the Russians were overrunning much of the Austro-Hungarian province of Galicia.

German Victories

Farther north, the Germans and Russians were fighting each other. In an attempt to help their ally France, the Russians attacked the German province of East Prussia in August, but they were defeated at the Battle of Tannenberg. The Russians restarted their offensive, this time aiming to strike farther south, from Russia's Polish

In 1914, the war on the Eastern Front was much more open than that on the Western Front.

KEY DATES

August 17, 1914 German troops defeat Russian invaders at Stallupönen, East Prussia.

August 24, 1914 German troops delay the Russian advance in East Prussia at the Battle of Orlau-Frankenau. They know the enemy's plans and gather at Tannenberg.

August 26, 1914 Germans attack the Russian Second Army at Tannenberg from the north and south and in the center.

August 29, 1914 By nightfall, the Russians are surrounded. Huge losses include 90,000 prisoners.

Continued on page 21

February 7 East Prussia Germans successfully attack Russian troops at the Second Battle of the Masurian Lakes.

March 1 Britain The British begin a naval blockade of Germany.

March

March 10 France The BEF launches an offensive at Neuve-Chapelle, using artillery fire to bombard enemy positions in preparation.

March 18 Mediterranean British and French vessels fail to force their way through thc Dardanelles by applying Allied naval power alone.

Battle of Tannenberg

On August 24, 1914, German troops successfully delayed the advance of Russian troops by a day in East Prussia. This gave the Germans time to concentrate at Tannenberg. The Russians did not realize that the Germans were listening to their radio messages and knew their plans. By August 29, the Germans had the Russian army surrounded. Tannenberg was a major German victory. The Russian losses were huge.

territories into the German area of Silesia. The Russian attack was halted by a German advance around Lódz in November. Many of the Germans had arrived by railroad from the Western Front.

The Great Retreat

The Russians defeated Austria-Hungary in early 1915, and the fortress of Przemysl surrendered. General Erich von Falkenhayn, the new German chief of the general staff, planned to focus on the Western Front, but Emperor Wilhelm II ordered him to give the Eastern Front priority. Von Falkenhayn therefore sent troops east. The German and Austro-Hungarian armies began their offensive around the towns of Gorlice and Tarnow in Galicia in May 1915. By the start of June, the

→ Cooks prepare food for German troops in the field during the defense of East Prussia.

TIMELINE **1915 APRIL–JUNE**

KEY: Western Front | Eastern Front | Other Fronts

April

April 5 France
A French attack in Meuse-Argonne makes little progress.

April 8 Turkey
Turks begin a massacre in which one million Armenians will die.

April 22 Belgium
Second Battle of Ypres. The Germans use poisonous gas for the first time, causing panic among British troops.

April 25 Turkey
Allied landings on the Gallipoli Peninsula fail to achieve their initial objectives.

April 26 Italy
Italy joins the war against its former ally, Austria-Hungary, in breach of a treaty.

May

May 7 Atlantic Ocean
A German submarine sinks the passenger liner *Lusitania*, killing many U.S. citizens.

Russian soldiers in Lódz await transportation to prison camps.

Continued from page 19

September 3, 1914 Russian Fifth Army splits two Austro-Hungarian armies at the Battle of Rava Ruska. By September 11, the Austro-Hungarians have lost 350,000 men.

September 7, 1914 Austro-Hungarian troops launch a second invasion of Serbia at the Battle of the Drina River.

September 9, 1914 Germans score a second major success as they surround Russian troops at the Masurian Lakes.

November 5–30, 1914 Renewed Austro-Hungarian attacks toward Belgrade see Serbian troops withdraw. Austro-Hungarian troops finally occupy the Serbian capital on December 2.

December 3–9, 1914 Serbian troops defeat the Austro-Hungarians at the Battle of Koluhra using extra ammunition sent by the French.

Germans had broken through. The Russians began what they called the "great retreat," which did not stop until the bad weather of the fall. By then, the Germans had advanced more than 300 miles (480 km). Czar Nicholas II, the Russian ruler, fired his top commander and took command of his forces himself.

Heavy Losses

The fighting in 1915 cost the Russians about one million troops killed and wounded, and another million taken prisoner. The Central Powers' successes also came at a price. Together, Germany and Austria-Hungary had about one million casualties on the Eastern Front. Late in 1915, Bulgaria joined the Central Powers and helped end Serbian resistance.

May 9 France
The British suffer heavy casualties at Neuve-Chapelle. The French open the Second Battle of Artois.

May 19 Turkey
Outnumbered Australians and New Zealanders defeat a Turkish attack at Gallipoli.

May 24 Belgium
There are heavy losses on both sides in the Second Battle of Ypres.

May 26 Britain
Naval chief Sir Winston Churchill is fired after the failure of his plans to knock Turkey out of the war at Gallipoli.

June

June 23–July Italy
First Battle of the Isonzo between the Italians and Austro-Hungarians sees heavy casualties and little progress.

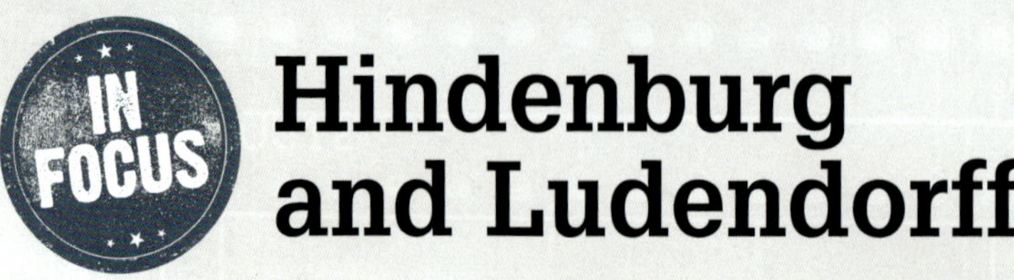

Hindenburg and Ludendorff

Calm and imperturbable, Paul von Hindenburg formed a good team with Erich von Ludendorff during World War I.

Hindenburg (1847–1934) and his deputy, Ludendorff (1865–1937), commanded the German armies in East Prussia in 1914. They saw that the attacking Russian forces could be defeated by using railroads to deploy the defending German units at key points on the flanks of the offensive. This enabled them to win the great victories of Tannenberg and the Masurian Lakes. In 1916, Hindenburg was appointed head of the whole German army, with Ludendorff as his chief of staff. Hindenburg was the calm, senior officer and Ludendorff the intellectual powerhouse.

Victory Slips Away

The two men enjoyed great victories in 1917, when the Russian army collapsed and Russia was forced to make peace. At the same time, they held off renewed French and British attacks on the Western Front. The French army was then beset by mutinies, and the two generals had moved Germany into a strong position. They knew, however, that the U.S. declaration of war meant they had to find victory swiftly. They ordered the Michael Offensive in 1918. This almost won a decisive victory on the Western Front. The Allies hung on, however, and finally Hindenburg accepted his army was beaten.

KEY DATES

October 2, 1847 Paul von Hindenburg is born in Posen (now Poznan), in what was then Prussia.

August 22, 1914 Hindenburg and Ludendorff take command of German armies in East Prussia facing a massive Russian invasion. They win the battles of Tannenberg and the Masurian Lakes.

1915 Hindenburg oversees an offensive that occupies what became the country of Poland and forces the Russian armies back.

1917 Hindenburg and Ludendorff are now in command of all German armies. They shorten the German lines on the Western Front, creating the so-called Hindenburg Line.

July 1918 Ludendorff suffers mental breakdown as the German Army Michael Offensive stalls on the Western Front.

August 2, 1934 Hindenburg dies in Neudeck in East Prussia (now Ogrodzieniec in Poland) while president of Germany. One of his final acts as president is to appoint Adolf Hitler chancellor of Germany in January 1933.

1 Hindenburg (left) and Ludendorff in 1914, during the operation that defeated the Russian armies and made their name.

2 Hindenburg (left) and Ludendorff (right) with Kaiser Wilhelm II (center) in a planning conference during the war.

3 Hindenburg in 1914, exhibiting his many decorations and with a classic Prussian officer's mustache.

4 Russian prisoners in 1914. The Russian army never really recovered from the string of defeats it suffered early in the war.

Failure at Gallipoli

The Ottoman Turks controlled the Dardanelles, which linked the Mediterranean with the Black Sea. The Allies wanted to seize the strait and defeat Turkey.

↑ A shell explodes near a pier used by the British to land troops and supplies at Gallipoli.

TIMELINE **1915 JULY–SEPTEMBER**

KEY: Western Front | Eastern Front | Other Fronts

July

July 9 Britain
Secretary of War Lord Kitchener calls for recruits. More than two million volunteer.

July 18 Italy
The Italians clash with Austro-Hungarians at the Second Battle of the Isonzo; it finishes on August 3 with few gains for either side.

August

August 4 Belgium
The Germans arrest British-born nurse Edith Cavell after she helps 200 prisoners of war escape. She is later executed.

August 6 Turkey
Allied troops land at Suvla Bay in Gallipoli to try to outflank the Turks; they are unable to move inland.

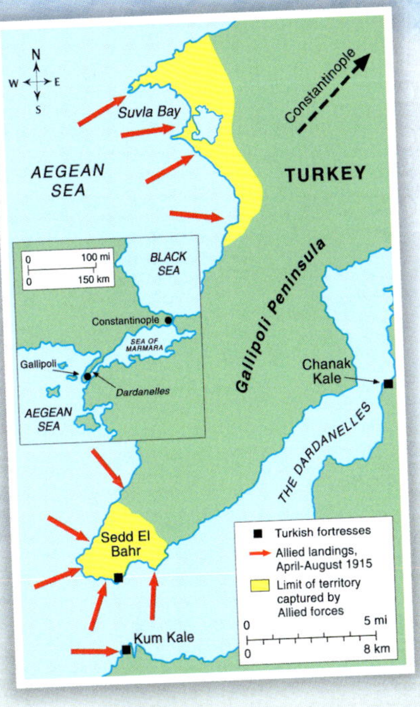

At the start of 1915, Britain's navy minister, Winston Churchill, convinced other Allied leaders to attack Turkey. He aimed to reopen the supply route to Russia through the Black Sea and to knock Germany's weakest partner out of the war. An Allied fleet bombarded Turkish forts on either side of the Dardanelles in February.

Naval Attack

A full-scale naval attack destroyed many of the Turkish coastal guns. Unknown to the Allies, however, the guns that were not damaged were low on ammunition. A sustained attack might have allowed Allied ships to sail to Constantinople (now Istanbul) and force the Turks to surrender. However, four Allied battleships struck mines and sank. The naval attack was called off.

Poor planning led to the Allies' defeat in the Gallipoli campaign.

KEY DATES

March 18, 1915 Final Anglo-French attempt fails to force a way through the Dardanelles by naval power alone.

April 25, 1915 Anglo-French invasion of the Gallipoli Peninsula begins badly. The Turks occupy the hilltops, from where they can fire down on the Allied troops landing on the beaches.

May 6, 1915 The British at Gallipoli fail to capture the town of Krithia and lose 6,500 soldiers in the process.

May 19, 1915 Australians and New Zealanders at Gallipoli—17,000 troops—defeat 40,000 Turkish soldiers, inflicting more than 3,000 casualties.

June 4, 1915 30,000 British troops fail for a second time to capture Krithia.

Continued on page 27

August 12 Britain Work starts on first tracked armored vehicle, or "tank."

September

September 18 Russia The Germans capture Vilna; in only a few months, they have forced the Russians to retreat 300 miles (480 km), out of Galicia and Poland.

September 25 France French attacks start the Second Battle of Champagne and the Battle of Artois. British attack in the Battle of Loos.

September 27–28 Mesopotamia The British successfully attack Turks at Kut-el-Amara on the Tigris River.

Mustafa Kemal

The Turkish resistance to the initial Anglo-French landings at Gallipoli was commanded by Mustafa Kemal. His energy and drive were key to avoiding Turkish defeat. Kemal became a hero to many Turks. After Turkey's defeat, he became head of an alternative Turkish government and led a march on the capital, Ankara, to drive out occupying forces. Kemal became president of the new Republic of Turkey in 1923. In 1934, he was given the name Ataturk, "Father of Turks."

After months of unsuccessful attacks and increasing casualties, the British leave Gallipoli.

Gallipoli

The Allies now decided to invade the Gallipoli Peninsula on the north side of the Dardanelles and advance on land toward the Turkish capital. However, it took weeks to get an invasion force ready. The Turks used the time to move defenders to the area. When the Allies began landing on April 25, the Turks had enough troops on the hills inland to hold them on the beaches. The Turkish commanders were helped by poor leadership and organization on the Allied side.

Australian troops advance with fixed bayonets against the Turkish trenches at Gallipoli.

TIMELINE 1915 OCTOBER–DECEMBER

KEY: Western Front | Eastern Front | Other Fronts

October

October 6 Serbia
German and Austro-Hungarian armies invade Serbia from the north; two Bulgarian armies invade from the east. The Serbian army retreats southwest.

October 6 France
The French launch a new offensive in the Second Battle of Champagne, but it runs out of steam with few gains.

October 13–14 France
The Battle of Loos ends with small British gains; within the army and in London, there is increasing criticism of the commander of the BEF, Sir John French.

The Allied troops, many of whom were from the Australia and New Zealand Army Corps (ANZAC), soon found what had been planned as a great strategic maneuver turned into a version of the Western Front. There were few alternatives to frontal attacks on tough enemy positions on hills overlooking the Allied trenches.

The Landings Abandoned

The Allies tried to restart their advance by making landings on an additional beachhead in August. The Turks were surprised, but poor British leadership again destroyed the slim chances of success.

A new British commander took over in October and recommended the landing force be evacuated. The evacuation operation was well planned. No Allied lives were lost during the two-stage withdrawal in December 1915 and January 1916. However, in the earlier fighting, each side had suffered about 250,000 casualties.

Continued from page 25

December 8, 1915
Evacuation of Allied positions begins at Suvla Bay and Ari Burna at Gallipoli. The Turks do not interfere. Some 83,000 people, 186 artillery pieces, and 1,700 vehicles, together with some 4,500 transport animals, are taken off the Gallipoli Peninsula by boat.

January 8, 1916 The Allied evacuation of the Gallipoli Peninsula is completed. The campaign has cost 252,000 British, Commonwealth, and French troops and the Turks around 250,000.

Indian troops crouch in shallow trenches as they defend the Suez Canal against the Turks.

November 10-December 2 Italy
Italians and Austro-Hungarians fight another inconclusive battle, the Fourth Battle of the Isonzo.

December 17 Britain
General Sir Douglas Haig becomes commander of the British Expeditionary Force in northern France.

November

December

November 22-26 Mesopotamia
British forces attack Turks at Ctesiphon but are forced to retreat to Kut-al-Amara.

December 3 France
General Joseph Joffre becomes commander in chief of all French forces on the Western Front.

December 8 Turkey
Turks fail to prevent Allied evacuation beginning at Gallipoli.

The War in Africa and Asia

Germany's colonies around the world were soon picked off by the Allies. Only in East Africa did the Germans fight on.

The largest battles of World War I were fought in Europe and the Middle East. There were also campaigns in East Asia and Africa, however. Japan entered the war on the side of the Allies in 1914 and a German colony in China was taken over by Japanese forces. Germany also had a colony in Samoa, which was invaded by New Zealand units.

Von Lettow-Vorbeck

In Africa, Germany had a number of colonies, most of which were soon occupied by the Allies. However, in German East Africa (covering an area comprising the present-day countries of Burundi, Rwanda, and Tanzania), the commander of the German forces led a stiff resistance. Paul von Lettow-Vorbeck commanded about 22,000 troops and managed to tie down over 250,000 Allied forces in a brilliant campaign that he kept going even after the end of the war in Europe.

KEY DATES

August 27, 1914 Japanese troops lay siege to the German-held city of Tsingtao (now Qingdao) in China. They take the city on November 7, 1914.

August 29, 1914 New Zealand forces take over German Samoa.

November 2, 1914 British forces attack the German base of Tanga in German East Africa. German commander Paul von Lettow-Vorbeck fights off this assault.

July 1915 British and South African troops under Jan Smuts and Louis Botha take over German Southwest Africa (now Namibia).

November 25, 1918 Von Lettow-Vorbeck surrenders his force to the British in East Africa. He has just 150 Germans and 1,200 African Askari soldiers under his command.

1 German troops in Tsingtao, the port they occupied in northern China. Tsingtao was besieged and taken by Allied forces.

2 November 1917: German Schutztruppe Askaris (locally raised forces) cross the Ruvuma River in Africa to break out of encirclement.

3 British troops disembark as they prepare to take part in the occupation of the German colony of Tsingtao in 1914.

4 A 1918 German poster celebrates the exploits of Paul von Lettow-Vorbeck.

The War at Sea

The war at sea between Britain and Germany was played out across the North Atlantic Ocean, where the Germans used U-boats (submarines) for the first time.

↑ German warships of the High Seas Fleet sail into the North Sea to confront the British at Jutland.

TIMELINE 1916 JANUARY–MARCH

KEY: Western Front | Eastern Front | Other Fronts

January

January 4 Mesopotamia
The British launch an attempt to relieve troops besieged by the Turks in Kut-al-Amara.

January 8 Turkey
Allies complete the evacuation of the Gallipoli Peninsula.

February

February 1 English Channel
German zeppelins bomb the British ship *Franz Fischer*, the first merchant ship ever sunk by air bombardment.

At the start of the war in 1914, Britain had the world's strongest navy and its largest merchant fleet. However, Germany had begun to build a strong navy of its own to threaten Britain's position. When the conflict began, Britain imposed a naval blockade. Within days of the war's start, almost all of Germany's merchant ships had been captured or had taken refuge in neutral ports.

Besides its larger fleet, Britain's geographical position blocked German access to the oceans. To reach the high seas, Germany had to defeat the Royal Navy. For Britain, defeat would mean that the war was lost. The responsibility for victory lay with the Grand Fleet's commander, Admiral John Jellicoe.

The Battle of Jutland

Only one large battle, the Battle of Jutland (the Battle of Skagerrak for the Germans), was fought between the two fleets, on May 31, 1916, in the North Sea, 50 miles (80 km) off the coast of Denmark. Despite having the upper hand early on, the Germans later retreated as Britain gained control.

KEY DATES

August 28, 1914 British and German vessels clash in the Battle of Heligoland Bight in the North Sea; the Germans lose four vessels.

September 22, 1914 The German submarine *U-9* sinks three British cruisers with the loss of 1,400 soldiers.

November 3, 1914 German warships in the North Sea bombard Britain's east coast. Raids peak on December 16, when the ports of Whitby and Hartlepool are attacked, causing more than 700 casualties.

December 8, 1914 The British sink four out of five German warships in an attack at the Battle of the Falkland Islands, in the south Atlantic off Argentina.

Continued on page 33

The engine room of a U-boat. Submarines were key to stopping supplies reaching France and Britain.

February 21 France Germans attack the strategically vital fortified town of Verdun using a huge artillery force.

February 22 France The French create a key supply road to Verdun, which comes to be called "the Sacred Way."

February 25 France The Germans take key French position at Verdun; General Henri-Philippe Pétain takes charge of French troops.

March

March 11 Italy The Fifth Battle of the Isonzo starts.

March 18 Russia Russians suffer heavy losses for little gain in the First Battle of Lake Naroch.

The Sinking of the *Lusitania*

On May 7, 1915, the German submarine *U-20* attacked the British passenger liner *Lusitania* as it sailed off the west coast of Ireland. In just 18 minutes, the ship sank, killing 1,198 people, including 128 Americans. A luxury liner, the *Lusitania* had sailed across the Atlantic without incident during the first months of the war. Its sinking caused outrage, especially in the United States, because it had come without warning. The incident was important to the United States declaring war on Germany.

After Jutland, the British blockade remained as effective as ever. The German fleet stayed in port for the rest of the war, contributing nothing to the war effort.

Submarine Warfare

World War I was the first conflict in which submarines were widely used. Germany's U-boats (*unterseeboots*) were a new technology, and their development before 1914 had been slow. In February 1915, Germany began to use them for its own blockade, sinking merchant ships carrying cargo to and from Britain. This period of submarine attacks lasted until September 1915.

The Germans renewed their attacks briefly in 1916, but stopped them after U.S. protests. However, they then decided that the danger of

➔ A German submarine crew watches an Italian merchant ship burn.

TIMELINE **1916 APRIL–JUNE**

KEY: Western Front | Eastern Front | Other fronts

April

April 9 France
The Germans capture French front-line trenches on "Dead Man" Ridge at Verdun.

April 21 Ireland
The Easter Rising. Irish nationalists, mainly in Dublin, launch a failed revolt against British authorities.

April 29 Mesopotamia
The besieged British surrender to the Turks at Kut-al-Amara.

May

The British liner *Lusitania* was sunk by a German submarine.

drawing the United States into the war was a risk they had to take and so resumed attacks.

The strategy nearly worked. U-boats sank more than 1,000 British ships in 1917. By May, Britain had only six weeks' supply of food. As a last resort, the British introduced a convoy system in which merchant ships crossed the Atlantic in groups guarded by escorting warships.

The tactic worked. British shipping losses in 1918 were less than half of those in 1917. The U-boat campaign had failed to starve Britain into defeat. Instead, it proved to be the main reason the United States joined the war in April 1917.

Continued from page 31

January 24, 1915 The Battle of the Dogger Bank sees a victory for Britain's faster and better-armed warships.

May 7, 1915 The liner *Lusitania* is sunk by the German submarine *U-20*; among the dead are 128 U.S. citizens.

May 31, 1916 In the Battle of Jutland (Skagerrak), the Germans sink three British battleships, three cruisers, and eight destroyers; the Germans lose one battleship, four cruisers, and five destroyers. Ultimately, however, the battle is a British victory that restricts the German High Fleet to its home ports.

March 18, 1917 Three U.S. vessels are sunk by German submarines. The incident further angers the United States.

Britain's HMS *Dreadnought* marked a new era in warship design.

May 13 Arabia
Arabs capture the Islamic holy city of Mecca from the Ottoman Turks.

May 27 United States
President Woodrow Wilson proposes an international body to maintain peace; this becomes the League of Nations.

May 31 North Sea
British and German fleets suffer losses at the Battle of Jutland.

June

June 4 Russia
Russia attacks Austro-Hungarians and Germans to coincide with a planned British attack on the Somme River in France.

June 7 France
After bitter fighting, the Germans capture Fort Vaux at Verdun.

June 17 Italy
Austro-Hungarians stop their Trentino Offensive as casualties get out of control.

The Italian Front

Italy entered the war in 1915, hoping for quick gains. These did not materialize.

Italy had been allied with Germany and Austria-Hungary before 1914. However, the Italian state had ambitions to take over parts of the Austro-Hungarian Empire, such as the city of Trieste, and refused to go to war. The Italian government engaged in secret talks with France and Britain, and in May 1915, Italy declared war on Austria-Hungary, and on Germany the next year.

Victory at Vittorio Veneto

Italy attacked Austria-Hungary through the Alps but suffered heavy losses during a series of battles across the Isonzo River. Then, in 1917, Italian forces were defeated by German Austro-Hungarian troops at the Battle of Caporetto in October and November. The victors could see Venice, but never reached the city. The Italian army managed to hang on, and the following year took the offensive, sweeping away the Austro-Hungarians.

1

LA DOMENICA DEL CORRIERE

Si pubblica a Milano ogni Domenica

Supplemento illustrato del "Corriere della Sera"

MILANO

24 Settembre - 1 ottobre 1916.

L'eroica fine del mutilato Enrico Toti: ferito per la terza volta, si alza e scaglia la sua gruccia contro il nemico in fuga.

2

3

KEY DATES

1912 Italy renews the Triple Alliance with Germany and Austria-Hungary, promising mutual support in the event of war.

May 22, 1915 Reneging on the Triple Alliance, Italy declares war on Austria-Hungary.

June 23, 1915 First Italian offensive on the Isonzo River. There will eventually be 17 failed offensives against Austro-Hungarian troops in this sector.

December 1917 Italian forces manage to stop German and Austro-Hungarian forces at the Battle of Monte Grappa, after the defeat at Caporetto.

October 24, 1918 Italian troops take the offensive in the Battle of Vittorio Veneto. The Austro-Hungarian army disintegrates and an armistice is signed on November 3.

1 In this heroic illustration of the struggle on the front lines, an Italian soldier urges his soldiers on despite having lost a leg.

2 Italian alpine troops slowly struggle up a mountainside in this more accurate photographic portrayal of war in the Alps.

3 Italian forces were thrown back at Caporetto in 1917. Here, some of the thousands of Italian prisoners are herded together.

4 Luigi Cadorna is the Italian general who ordered many of the suicidal offensives on the Isonzo front.

5 Trench warfare in the Alps. At an altitude of 12,000 feet (3,850 m), this may have been the highest trench ever dug in the war.

The Struggle at Verdun

By 1916, it was clear there were no quick victories to be won on the Western Front. The Germans chose to attack the fortified town of Verdun, on the border with France.

The painting *The Ravine of the Dead* captures the horrors of the fighting around Verdun in 1916.

TIMELINE **1916 JULY–SEPTEMBER**

KEY: Western Front | Eastern Front | Other Fronts

July

July 1 France
British Somme Offensive starts. British casualties of 60,000 is greatest loss ever in a single day's combat.

July 4 Germany
German naval chiefs suggest using submarines against British merchant ships.

July 10 Russia
Russians have captured 300,000 prisoners since the so-called Brusilov Offensive started.

August

August 4 Italy
The Sixth Battle of the Isonzo fails to end a stalemate.

Verdun, about 120 miles (192 km) east of Paris, was a major strongpoint on the French border. German chief of staff Erich von Falkenhayn guessed correctly that the French would commit everything to hold it.

A Slogging Match

The attack began on February 21, 1916. After four days, the Germans captured Fort Douaumont. They believed they had won a great victory. In fact, the French high command had decided to hold Verdun despite the loss of the fort. Reinforcements were arriving, and a new commander, General Henri-Philippe Pétain, reorganized the French, who began to use their artillery more effectively. The battlefield became a scene of slaughter on both sides, but gradually the German front line crept forward. Pétain

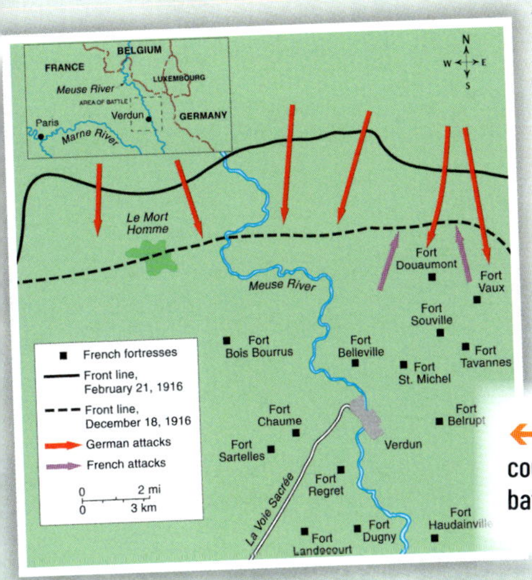

The Germans believed they could win at Verdun, but the battle ended in a stalemate.

KEY DATES

February 21, 1916 The German offensive begins. The main attack is by 140,000 troops of Crown Prince William's Fifth Army. The French are pushed back.

February 22, 1916 The French create *La Voie Sacrée* ("The Sacred Way"). This narrow road to Verdun becomes the main route for supplies and reinforcements entering the city. Around Verdun, German attacks gain some ground but are met by fierce French counterattacks.

February 25, 1916 One of the key French positions at Verdun, Fort Douaumont, falls to Germans. General Pétain takes charge of French troops.

June 7, 1916 After weeks of bitter fighting, the Germans capture Fort Vaux from the French.

Continued on page 39

September

August 29 Germany
Field Marshal Paul von Hindenburg becomes chief of the general staff; General Erich Ludendorff becomes his deputy.

September 15 France
Using tanks for the first time on the Western Front, the British break the deadlock on the Somme by capturing the villages of Flers and Courcelette.

September 17 France
German air ace Baron Manfred von Richthofen scores his first victory.

General Henri-Philippe Pétain

After the start of war, Pétain was so good at his job that he quickly rose through the ranks until he took command at Verdun in 1916. Pétain made sure that his soldiers had food and medical care. That ended their frequent mutinies and ensured the French could fight into 1918. However, after World War II, Pétain was tried as a traitor for cooperating with the Nazis during that war.

was promoted, and Robert Nivelle took his place as commander of the French Second Army at Verdun.

Attack After Attack

By early June 1916, the Germans were pushing forward again. Verdun seemed certain to fall. Pétain—or possibly Nivelle—issued special orders, which included France's most famous slogan of the war: "*Ils ne passeront pas!*" ("They shall not pass!"). Somehow, the French held on.

On July 1, the British began their attack on the Somme River sector. The Germans withdrew troops from Verdun in order to reinforce their defenses there. Attacks and counterattacks at Verdun continued until Field Marshal Paul von Hindenburg and General Erich Ludendorff, who took over the German army in

➔ *Le Mort Homme Ridge* (Dead Man Ridge) at Verdun shows the results of prolonged artillery fire.

TIMELINE 1916 OCTOBER–DECEMBER

KEY: Western Front | Eastern Front | Other Fronts

October

October 7 United States
Woodrow Wilson is reelected to a second term as president.

October 10 Russia
Czar Nicholas orders the end of the successful Brusilov Offensive.

October 16 Arabia
British captain T. E. Lawrence ("Lawrence of Arabia") becomes an adviser to Prince Feisal, who is leading an Arab revolt against the Turks.

French soldiers on their way to Verdun along the Sacred Way, a vital supply line.

August, halted all German attacks at Verdun. Both realized that the plan to destroy the French army had little chance of success.

The French counterattack recaptured Fort Douaumont on October 24 and regained much of the ground they had lost. Their attacks continued until the battle was halted on December 18. In the last days, the French captured nearly 120,000 Germans.

About one million soldiers had been killed or wounded, just over half of them on the French side. But little had been achieved. Both sides were back where they had started by the close of the fighting. Erich von Falkenhayn had hoped to smash the French army, but both armies had suffered equally. Neither side could claim victory.

Continued from page 37

June 22, 1916 The Germans attack again, using a new type of poison gas that the French gas masks do not protect against.

October 24, 1916 The French attack northeast of Verdun. They retake Fort Douaumont, with 6,000 prisoners.

December 15, 1916 The French attack to the northeast of Verdun. Within a few days, they force the Germans away from key positions, including Forts Douaumont and Vaux. The attack ends the main Battle of Verdun. Losses are huge: 360,000 French troops and 336,000 German troops. The German plan to destroy the French army has failed.

General Pétain was one of France's greatest war heroes.

November

December

December 5 Britain Prime Minister Herbert Asquith resigns and is replaced by David Lloyd George.

December 6 Romania The Germans enter Bucharest.

December 13 Mesopotamia A British offensive begins along the Tigris River; progress is slow.

December 15 France The Battle of Verdun ends. Losses on both sides have been huge, but the French have managed to hang on.

Slaughter on the Somme

British forces, helped by troops from Commonwealth countries, took the leading Allied role in the bloody Battle of the Somme in 1916. Many lost their lives.

British troops rest near a Mark I tank during a lull in the fighting on the Somme.

TIMELINE **1917 JANUARY–MARCH**

KEY: Western Front | Eastern Front | Other Fronts

January

January 19 Mexico
British decode the Zimmerman telegram, a suggested German alliance with Mexico if the U.S. declares war on Germany.

January 31 Germany
The Germans launch unrestricted submarine warfare.

February

February 3 United States
The United States cuts diplomatic ties with Germany over unrestricted submarine warfare.

The British role in the Somme Offensive was increased because French troops were preoccupied by the struggle at Verdun. The Somme River region was chosen because it was where the two Allied armies met, not because it was a good place to attack. The Germans held strong defensive positions on high ground overlooking the Allied lines.

Using Artillery

Key to the plans of British general Douglas Haig was a huge amount of artillery and shells. The British believed that they had assembled enough supplies at the Somme for a decisive barrage. They were wrong. More than one quarter of the shells did not explode, and those that did were poor at blasting gaps in barbed wire and useless for smashing defensive positions, the prime purposes of the artillery bombardment.

KEY DATES

June 24, 1916 The British begin shelling German trenches around the Somme River. Some 1.7 million shells are fired on the first day, but they fail to destroy German barbed wire or their strongly constructed defenses.

July 1, 1916 The Somme Offensive begins. The attacking British infantry are confronted by uncut German barbed wire and intact defenses and meet a wall of machine-gun fire. Casualties are the greatest ever suffered by the British in a single day's fighting.

July 14, 1916 A British advance almost breaks through German lines, but reserves arrive too late.

Continued on page 43

The British advanced only 6 miles (10 km) and suffered 400,000 casualties.

February 23 France Germans withdraw to the newly built Hindenburg Line, 20 miles (32 km) behind the existing line.

March 12 Russia Revolutionaries and the Russian parliament establish rival governments, in the start of a power struggle.

March 18 Atlantic Ocean German submarines sink three U.S. vessels.

March

March 8 Russia Demonstrations in Moscow against food and fuel shortages; based on the Russian calendar then in use, the event is usually called the "February Revolution."

March 15 Russia Czar Nicholas II abdicates.

March 26 Palestine First Battle of Gaza sees the initial British invasion of Turkish-held Palestine fail to make progress.

Field Marshal Sir Douglas Haig

Douglas Haig was the commander in chief of the British troops on the Western Front from December 1915 to the end of the war. After planning and leading the major British offensives at the Somme in 1916, he was promoted to field marshal, despite the attack's failure. Haig was a skilled organizer who worked well with his French allies. But Haig was criticized for the high number of casualties he lost in the battle he planned.

A British mine explodes underneath the German trenches near Beaumont Hamel.

Disaster on Day One

Following the artillery bombardment, the British infantry climbed out of their trenches to advance. But the German front lines remained intact. The British were mowed down, many before they had gone more than a few yards. Some of them got across no-man's land, only to find the German barbed wire still in place. As they tried to find a way through, many more soldiers were machine-gunned down. Almost 20,000 British soldiers died on July 1, 1916, and another 40,000 were wounded. It was a disastrous day for the British army.

British troops advance toward German lines in the Battle of the Somme.

TIMELINE 1917 APRIL–JUNE

KEY: Western Front | Eastern Front | Other Fronts

April

April 3 Russia
Revolutionary Vladimir Lenin returns from exile and starts plans to take control of Russia.

April 6 United States
The United States declares war on Germany.

April 9 France
British troops under Douglas Haig make good gains in the Battle of Arras.

April 16–20 France
General Robert Nivelle launches a major French offensive in Champagne and along the Aisne River; having captured plans for the attack, the Germans defeat the advance easily.

April 17 France
French troops mutiny, angry at futile offensives.

The Stationary Front Lines

In the weeks that followed, there were many chances for both sides to get the upper hand, but they were missed. There were no portable radios to quickly pass messages, and so it took hours to carry out orders or maneuvers, giving the enemy time to rebuild their positions. Despite some small gains on both sides, the front lines remained largely stationary.

Ending the Battle

On September 15, 1916, the British used their new secret weapon, the tank, for the first time ever in the Battle of Flers-Courcelette. The tanks were clumsy and unreliable. The British captured some ground, but by the end of the day, hardly any of the tanks were working. By the end of the battle, the British had advanced no more than 6 miles (10 km) from their starting positions. Some 125,000 British Empire troops had died in the process, along with 50,000 French. No one knows how many Germans died: estimates range from about 100,000 to 160,000. For every man killed on each side, roughly three more were wounded. Neither side achieved a clear victory in the bloody Battle of the Somme.

Continued from page 41

August 1, 1916 The Somme Offensive is a month old: British casualties total 158,000; German losses are 160,000.

September 15, 1916 The British begin an offensive to break the deadlock; tanks appear on the Western Front for the first time. The British capture two villages, Flers and Courcelette, but the slow-moving tanks are not a success, although they initially panic German troops.

November 18, 1916 The Battle of the Ancre marks the end of the British offensive on the Somme. At the end of their attacks, the British have still not captured some of their initial objectives.

Haig led British forces on the Western Front.

May

June

May 9 France
General Nivelle's offensive fails, with heavy casualties.

May 10 Britain
Lloyd George orders British Royal Navy to accompany merchant ships in convoy to protect them. Merchant ship sinkings fall.

May 23 Britain
German bombers attack London from their bases in occupied Belgium.

June 7 Belgium
British forces capture the Messines Ridge, which allows the offensive of Passchendaele, or Third Battle of Ypres.

The War in the Air

In 1914, a new dimension entered warfare as aircraft brought the struggle into the clouds.

World War I was the first major conflict in which aerial warfare played a major role. While there had been attempts to use balloons and similar technology previously in warfare, it was in 1914 that there was a sudden need to take command of the air. The importance of gaining control of the air was clear to all.

There were three major areas of fighting in the air. Balloons, which had been used for reconnaissance in previous wars, were important for artillery spotting. Attacking enemy balloons and defending friendly ones became an important role for aircraft. Small agile aircraft also fought each other to gain control of the skies. These were usually biplanes (with two pairs of wings) although one of the most successful aircraft was the German Fokker triplane, with three pairs of wings.

Bombing

The third major aspect of aerial warfare came later in the war. Larger machines were developed that could drop bombs on enemy positions or enemy cities. These consisted of heavier-than-air aircraft and powered balloons such as the German zeppelins.

KEY DATES

1911 Italian planes drop improvised bombs in the first use of fixed-wing aircraft in war during the invasion of Libya.

August 5, 1914 A German zeppelin drops bombs on the French city of Liege. It is damaged by defensive fire, crash lands, and is destroyed.

September 8, 1914 First deadly aerial combat. A Russian pilot rams an Austro-Hungarian plane and both machines crash.

July 1915 A synchronized, forward-firing machine gun, able to fire between the blades of a turning propeller and fitted to a German Fokker monoplane, revolutionizes aerial warfare. It gives German pilots an advantage for a time.

April 21, 1918 Death of Manfred von Richtofen, the most successful German air ace of the war, with 80 victories in aerial dogfights.

September 12, 1918 Beginning of Battle of Saint-Mihiel. The U.S. Air Service deploys almost 1,500 aircraft in support of the successful offensive, the largest air operation of the war.

1 A recruiting poster for the U.S. Air Service, issued after the declaration of war by President Woodrow Wilson in 1917.

2 A Sopwith F1 Camel. This biplane was the most successful British fighter of the war.

3 U.S. DH-4 bombers in formation during 1918. By then, aerial combat and close air support for ground troops were standard.

4 Fokker triplanes. The Fokker was one of the best fighter planes of the war.

5 A Fokker DR-1 unit of the German Air Force. Fokker made a range of aircraft, from monoplanes to triplanes.

A Pivotal Year

Both sides began 1917 with new plans for the Western Front. The French and British planned major offensives for the spring to crush the Germans.

Canadian troops start to dig in after their victory on Vimy Ridge.

TIMELINE **1917 JULY–SEPTEMBER**

KEY: Western Front | Eastern Front | Other Fronts

July

July 18 Belgium
The British begin a preliminary bombardment before their planned attack in the region of Ypres.

July 24 France
Dutch dancer Mata Hari stands trial as a German spy; she is later found guilty and executed.

July 31 Belgium
Third Battle of Ypres begins. It soon grinds to a halt.

August

August 2 Belgium
The British offensive at Ypres is temporarily halted after rain turns the ground to mud; the offensive resumes on August 16, when the ground is drier.

August 2 Russia
General Lavr Kornilov replaces Aleksey Brusilov as Russia's commander in chief.

After the terrible casualties suffered by the German army in 1916, General Erich Ludendorff decided on a new strategy for 1917. He ordered the German army to stop counterattacking every Allied advance. He also withdrew his troops from a large area of captured French territory to a strong new defensive system, the Hindenburg Line, from which he would attack the Allied forces. The German retreat forced a French change of plan.

The French Mutinies

In April 1917, French commander Robert Nivelle launched a new offensive, the Second Battle of the Aisne, but it rapidly stalled. The French

KEY DATES

April 9, 1917 The British begin the Battle of Arras to try to force a German withdrawal from the Aisne River sector, which the French are about to attack; they make gains on the first day but lose many aircraft shot down by the Germans.

April 11, 1917 The Battle of Arras becomes a stalemate as German resistance grows; by the time it ends in mid-May, British casualties are 150,000 and German casualties are 100,000.

April 16–20, 1917 General Nivelle's French offensive along the Aisne River fails because Germans know of his plans in advance.

April 17, 1917 Nivelle's troops mutiny and abandon their posts.

May 9, 1917 Nivelle's offensive fails; the French have suffered huge losses: 187,000 versus German losses of 163,000.

Continued on page 49

Woodrow Wilson requests U.S. Congress to support war with Germany.

September

September 1 Russia German stormtroopers capture the town of Riga; many Russian soldiers simply desert their posts.

September 20 Belgium The focus of the British offensives at Ypres switches to the south of the region.

September 27–28 Mesopotamia After defeating the Turks at the Battle of Ramadi, the British pursue them deep into central Mesopotamia.

Tanks

The British had developed tanks from farm tractors that were fitted with caterpillar tracks to prevent them sinking into the ground. The new weapons were first used on a large scale at Cambrai in November 1917. Although the tanks were unreliable, they could create gaps in the German lines. The Germans later built their own tanks, but mainly used British tanks recovered from various battlefields.

soldiers had had enough. In addition to their losses, they had to put up with awful food, almost no leave, and poor medical services. In April 1917, thousands mutinied. Nivelle was fired and replaced by General Henri-Philippe Pétain, who addressed the soldiers' concerns and ended the mutinies.

Passchendaele

In July 1917, Douglas Haig launched an offensive around the Belgian town of Ypres after a long artillery barrage. Even though the British had more artillery and air superiority, ground conditions and weather favored the defense. Torrential rain fell as artillery shells turned the battlefield into a swamp. The British attacked until mid-November, when they switched their target to the village of Passchendaele. They lost about 300,000 casualties for only a 5-mile (8 km) advance.

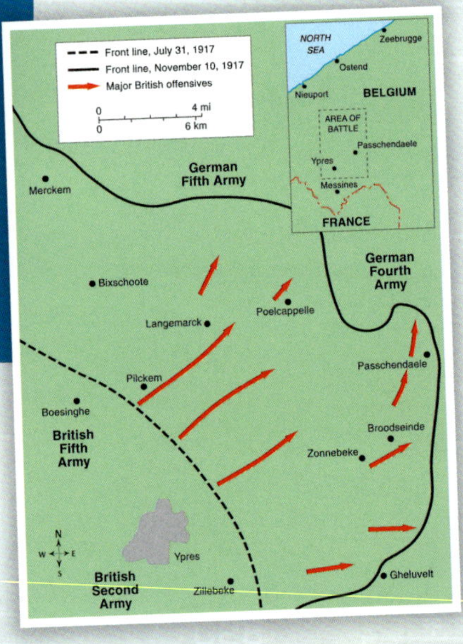

➔ The Battle of Passchendaele was the British army's major offensive in 1917.

TIMELINE 1917 OCTOBER–DECEMBER

KEY: Western Front | Eastern Front | Other Fronts

October

October 12 Belgium
British offensive at Ypres switches to Passchendaele.

October 24 Italy
The Austro-Hungarians launch the Twelfth Battle of the Isonzo (Battle of Caporetto), taking ground from the Italians.

October 26 Belgium
The new British offensive is aimed at Passchendaele.

November

November 6 Belgium
The British finally capture Passchendaele after hard-fought fighting.

An aerial view of the Nivelle Offensive. It was France's only major attack in 1917.

Massed Tank Attack

The Battle of Cambrai in November was the world's first tank-led battle. Some 320 British tanks smashed a gap in the German lines, but over half broke down or were destroyed on the first day. With no reserves, the British were pushed back.

The year ended with the armies on the Western Front suffering huge casualties for little apparent gain.

Continued from page 47

June 7, 1917 British troops capture Messines Ridge in southwest Belgium, paving the way for the Battle of Passchendaele, or the Third Battle of Ypres.

July 31, 1917 The battle begins with British advances of just 2 miles (3 km).

October 12, 1917 The British focus at Ypres switches to the village of Passchendaele.

November 6, 1917 The British finally take Passchendaele; casualties on both sides are high.

November 20, 1917 The Battle of Cambrai is the first major tank-led battle in history.

British troops attempt to free a light field gun from the mud at Ypres.

December

November 13–15 Palestine
British troops break through Turkish defenses at the Battle of Junction Station.

November 20 France
The first big tank battle of the war, the Battle of Cambrai, begins.

December 5 France
The Battle of Cambrai ends; it suggested that massed tanks could lead a breakout on the Western Front.

December 9 Palestine
The British take Jerusalem as the Turks abandon the city.

The Russian Revolution

Revolution in Russia changed the calculations of all the other World War I combatants.

Ever since August 1914, the Russian Empire had suffered heavy losses during the war. Even successful Russian offensives such as the Brusilov Offensive in 1916 had resulted in huge Russian casualty figures. In February 1917, the patience of the Russian people finally snapped. There were mutinies and in that month, Czar Nicholas II abdicated. A provisional government was put in place and local revolutionary committees known as Soviets began forming all over the country. Russia was in turmoil.

Bolshevik Victory

The war continued to go badly, however, and in October a group of communist revolutionaries known as the Bolsheviks took over the government in the capital, Petrograd (now St. Petersburg). The following March, they signed the Treaty of Brest-Litovsk with Germany, and Russia stopped fighting Germany. This enabled the German high command to move troops to the Western Front to undertake a major offensive there. Russia, meanwhile, descended into civil war as Bolsheviks fought against their enemies within Russia in a struggle between the Reds (Bolsheviks) and Whites (a combination of anti-Bolshevik and nationalist groups). In spite of anti-Bolshevik intervention from countries such as Britain, the Reds eventually won this war in 1923.

KEY DATES

April 1917 Bolshevik leader Vladimir Ilyich Lenin returns to Russia in a train provided by the Germans, with whom Russia is at war.

July 1917 Alexander Kerensky becomes head of the Provisional Government that had replaced the czar in February that year. Kerensky decides to carry on the war, which is now unpopular. Lenin masterminds a coup in October 1917 in Petrograd that brings the Bolsheviks to power.

January 1918 Leon Trotsky creates the Red Army to fight the anti-Bolshevik forces (the Whites).

July 16, 1918 The Russian royal family, the Romanovs, are murdered by Bolsheviks in the town of Yekaterinburg.

August 1920 Bolshevik forces moving west are halted outside Warsaw.

1923 Final White forces surrender near Vladivostok. The Bolsheviks control all Russia.

1 Leon Trotsky, a dynamic organizer, created the Red Army that fought the long civil war against the Whites.

2 The Petrograd Soviet in 1917. Soviets (committees) were set up all over Russia by those wanting to create a new government.

3 Demonstrators flee as they are fired on by soldiers on Nevsky Prospect, the main street in Petrograd. The czar abdicated in February 1917.

4 Anti-Bolshevik troops, Whites, during the long Russian Civil War.

5 A French magazine carries the story of the massacre of the imperial family by Bolsheviks in Yekaterinburg.

Germany's Last Gamble

At the start of 1918, Germany was in a bad position. American troops were on the way to Europe. The Germans planned one last offensive before they arrived.

British and French troops hastily built defenses at the start of Operation Michael.

TIMELINE 1918 JANUARY–MARCH

KEY: Western Front | Eastern Front | Other Fronts

January

January 8 United States
President Wilson outlines his Fourteen Points, a peace program to end the war.

January 27 Mesopotamia
With Russia in turmoil after the revolution, a British force sets out to take control of Russian oil wells on the Caspian Sea.

February

February 18 Russia
Irritated by Bolshevik delays in peace negotiations, German forces move deeper into Russia.

Stormtroopers on the march at the beginning of Operation Michael.

General Erich Ludendorff correctly realized the Allies' greatest weakness was that they did not always work together. The French priority was to guard Paris, while the British wanted to defend northern France and the English Channel. In March 1918, Ludendorff planned Operation Michael: an attack on Amiens in France with the aim of dislodging the British and driving the French south.

To achieve his plan, Ludendorff trained stormtroopers, elite infantry, to advance after the initial bombardment. However, since stormtroopers received the best rations and weapons, morale in the rest of the German army started to fall.

KEY DATES

March 21, 1918 Operation Michael begins with German stormtroopers easily overwhelming British troops.

March 23, 1918 The Germans begin the bombardment of Paris that will last until August 9.

March 27, 1918 German troops are close to Amiens, but their attack is stopped by Allied troops 10 miles (16 km) to the east.

April 5, 1918 Operation Michael is halted; the Germans have advanced 40 miles (64 km), but both sides have suffered heavy casualties.

April 9–10, 1918 Ludendorff opens Operation Georgette. The Germans win early gains.

Continued on page 55

March

March 3 Russia
Bolsheviks fighting a civil war are forced to give up territory in the Brest-Litovsk peace treaty with the Germans.

March 21 France
General Ludendorff launches Operation Michael, planned as a knockout blow before U.S. troops arrive on the Western Front.

March 23 France
The Germans start the bombardment of Paris. Shelling lasts until August 9.

March 29 France
U.S. ace Eddie Rickenbacker scores his first kill; by the end of the war, he will have 26 air victories.

Stormtroopers in World War I

The role of Germany's elite stormtroopers was to penetrate as deeply and quickly into enemy territory as they could. The first wave made no attempt to capture frontline enemy strongpoints. They bypassed them for follow-up troops to deal with. The tactic was also used to great effect at the start of World War II in 1939.

The German attack began on March 21, 1918. By the end of the first day, the British were in retreat with 20,000 soldiers taken prisoner. By March 25, the Germans had advanced about 25 miles (40 km), farther and faster than in any other battle.

The next day, the Allies appointed General Ferdinand Foch to coordinate operations on the Western Front. The Allies began to work together more effectively. Seeing that further efforts to drive them apart were useless, Ludendorff halted the offensive on April 5.

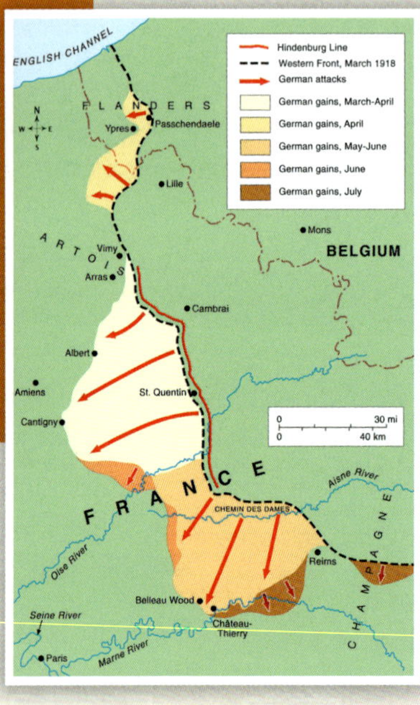

The Germans advanced across a wide front, but they were ultimately halted.

Renewed Attacks

Soon Ludendorff began a new attack, this time around Ypres in Belgium. Operation Georgette began on April 9 but again Allied defenses held it up after initial gains. Ludendorff still believed the British were his toughest opponents, but he did not want to attack them until he had drawn Allied reserves south. He moved his artillery and his remaining stormtroopers

TIMELINE 1918 APRIL–JUNE

KEY: Western Front | Eastern Front | Other Fronts

April

April 5 France
General Ludendorff orders a halt on Operation Michael.

April 9–10 France/Belgium
Ludendorff launches Operation Georgette, an offensive along the Lys River aimed at the English Channel ports through which Britain receives supplies.

April 17 France/Belgium
British and French troops halt the Lys River offensive near Ypres.

April 21 Western Front
German pilot Baron Manfred von Richthofen is shot down and killed. He was the most successful air ace of the war.

south to the Chemin des Dames area of the Aisne River sector, where he launched an attack on May 27. Helped by poor defensive tactics, the Germans defeated the Allies along a 25-mile (40 km) front.

American Arrival

At this point newly arrived U.S. troops played a key part in the fighting. The U.S. Third Division halted a German advance at Château-Thierry, across the Marne. The U.S. Second Division suffered heavy casualties but helped drive the Germans back in the Battle of Belleau Wood, which was captured after three weeks. Ludendorff knew he had to attack to keep the advantage. He began an offensive along the Marne, but was pushed back by Allied counterattacks. On August 8, thousands of German troops began to surrender. It was now clear that Germany could not win the war.

Continued from page 53

April 17, 1918 British and French troops around Ypres halt a German advance toward the ports of northern France; both sides have losses amounting to around 100,000.

April 23, 1918 The British launch a surprise amphibious assault on the Belgian ports of Ostend and Zeebrugge to stop German submarines operating in the English Channel, but the raid is a failure.

May 28, 1918 U.S. forces make their first attack of the war around Cantigny, which they capture but for the loss of 1,600 men.

June 5, 1918 Ludendorff halts all German attacks.

June 6, 1918 U.S. forces attack at Belleau Wood, which they capture after three weeks of fighting; U.S. losses are 1,800 killed and 7,000 wounded.

German howitzers during Operation Michael

May 28 France
U.S. forces in France undertake their first attack at Cantigny.

June 4 France
Ludendorff calls off his latest offensive, which has run out of steam.

May

June

May 27 France
Ludendorff launches a third offensive of the year, this time on the Aisne River; the Germans advance 10 miles (16 km) on the first day.

June 6 France
U.S. forces attack at Belleau Wood. It takes three weeks of hard fighting to capture it.

June 15–22 Italy
In the Battle of the Piave River, the Italians halt and then turn back an Austro-Hungarian advance.

U.S. Pressure Counts

Simultaneous Allied offensives drove the Germans back on the Western Front. One of these was the Meuse-Argonne Offensive, the largest U.S. action of the war.

As the Allies advanced, they took large numbers of German prisoners.

TIMELINE 1918 JULY–SEPTEMBER

KEY: Western Front | Eastern Front | Other Fronts

July

July 15–17 France
French troops are ready for a major German offensive along the Marne River and stop the German advance.

July 16–17 Russia
Bolsheviks murder the Russian royal family, including Czar Nicholas II.

July 18 France
The Second Battle of the Marne sees French, British, and U.S. forces attack; German defenses collapse.

August

August 6 France
The Second Battle of the Marne ends disastrously for the Germans.

The offensive began on September 26, 1918, and was the first mainly U.S. battle of the war. It was a key test of the policy of U.S. commander John Pershing in keeping his own forces separate from those of France and Britain and under his direct command. If the offensive failed, American enthusiasm for the war might be blunted, and the Germans could hope for a more favorable treaty to end the war.

The Offensive Stalls

The offensive aimed to drive the Germans away from the defenses of the Hindenburg Line. In its path lay the Argonne, a forested landscape of steep slopes and tree-covered ridges. Well-guarded river valleys, including the Meuse, pierced the forest. About 600,000 Allied troops took part in the offensive, which made good initial gains.

U.S. artillery opens fire on the enemy at Meuse-Argonne.

KEY DATES

September 12-16, 1918
The American Expeditionary Corps, with French II Colonial Corps, attacks German-held St. Mihiel; German resistance collapses, and U.S. troops capture 15,000 prisoners at a cost of 7,000 casualties.

September 26, 1918
The U.S. First Army—of one million—launches the Meuse-Argonne Offensive; the first five days bring rapid gains.

September 30, 1918
The offensive halts as U.S. troops become gridlocked on forest roads.

October 3, 1918 At the end of the first phase of the advance, two of three German defensive lines have been taken.

October 4, 1918 The second phase of the battle begins; many U.S. troops are veterans of the St. Mihiel battle.

Continued on page 59

September

August 8 France
The British lead the Amiens Offensive. Many German troops flee or surrender.

September 12-16 France
The American Expeditionary Corps, with a French colonial corps, captures the salient at St. Mihiel, held by the Germans since 1914.

September 19-21 Palestine
The British defeat the Turks at the Battle of Meggido.

September 26-October 3 France
One million U.S. troops launch the Meuse-Argonne Offensive. They make rapid gains.

Black Americans

The U.S. Army was still segregated by color. Although Black Americans made up some 13 percent of the troops in France, they were often made to do only menial support jobs. Those Black Americans who reached the front line proved to be courageous fighters. Despite many instances of bravery, however, no Black American was awarded the Congressional Medal of Honor.

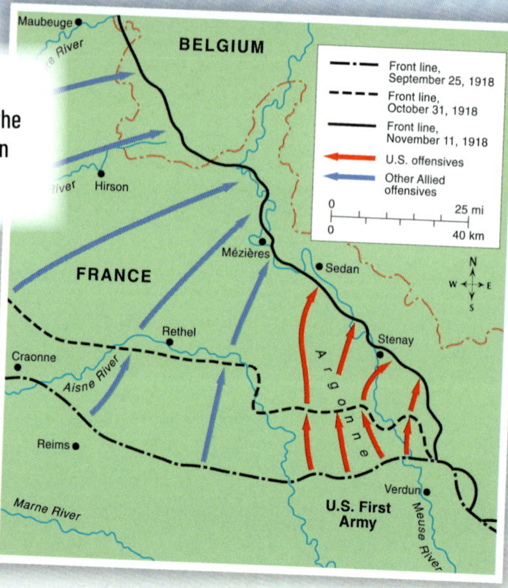

➔ The Argonne was a key point in the German defenses on the Western Front.

However, things soon began to go wrong. The troops were too inexperienced to keep to coordinated plans in such difficult terrain, and units soon fell behind. Some infantry attacks had little support and suffered heavy casualties. Pershing tried to send in reserves, but this only made matters worse. The roads leading into the battle area became gridlocked. Many of the reserves could not get into battle, and some frontline units were left without supplies. By September 30, after gaining about 10 miles (16 km), the offensive had to be halted.

The Final Breakthrough

The second phase of the attack started on October 4. This time, many of the frontline troops were made up of veterans of St. Mihiel. Strong

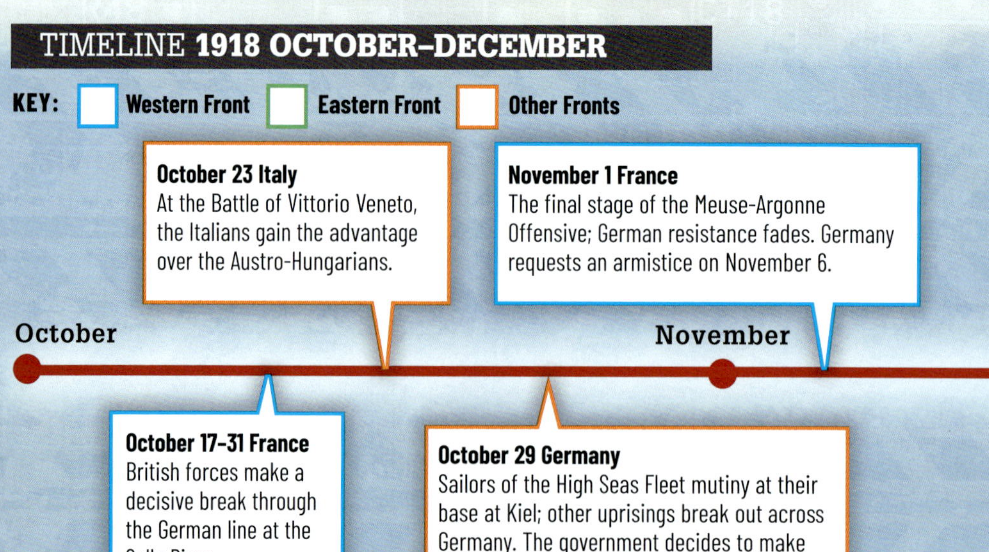

German defenses meant that progress was still slow, but the terrain often left the Americans little option other than to batter straight ahead at the enemy.

At the end of October, the U.S. advance finally reached more open ground. The German front began to crack. By the time World War I finally came to an end on November 11, most of the U.S. objectives had been reached. It had been a costly process, however. The 117,000 casualties were almost half of the total U.S. losses for the whole war.

Continued from page 57

October 26, 1918 The third phase of the battle begins.

October 27, 1918 Ludendorff resigns as Germany's chief military planner, clearing the way for the German government to agree to an end to the fighting with the Allies.

October 31, 1918 U.S. forces have cleared the Argonne Forest and move into more open country; they are reorganized into two armies.

November 11, 1918 When the armistice comes into effect at 11:00 a.m., U.S. troops are still engaged at Meuse-Argonne. They have achieved most of their goals but at a high price; the offensive has the highest death toll of any single battle in U.S. history.

Parisians celebrate the armistice on the Western Front, November 11, 1918.

November 3 Austria-Hungary The Austro-Hungarians seek an armistice with Italy, which is agreed to the next day.

November 9 Germany Kaiser Wilhelm II abdicates.

November 11 Europe The armistice comes into force at 11:00 a.m.; World War I is over.

December

December 1 Germany British, French, and U.S. forces move into the Rhineland as part of the armistice terms.

December 13 France President Woodrow Wilson arrives for the Paris peace talks—the first U.S. president to travel abroad.

Woodrow Wilson: The Versailles Treaty

Although an armistice ended the fighting on the Western Front, there were years of negotiations to come.

President Woodrow Wilson had reluctantly led the United States into World War I. He made a speech in January 1918 in which he outlined his so-called Fourteen Points for a new world order after the war. He wanted to set up an international organization to prevent future world wars, and he also firmly believed in the establishment of new national states for peoples such as the Poles and the Czechs who were ruled by foreign powers.

Further Warfare

At the Paris Peace Conference of 1919, Wilson proposed a new organization, the League of Nations, to mediate and prevent war. He also helped set up new countries. However, he was unable to stop Britain and France from making Germany pay punitive reparations through the Treaty of Versailles, signed in June 1919. When Wilson returned to the United States, Congress refused to ratify the Treaty of Versailles.

The Versailles Treaty ended World War I between the western Allies and Germany, but the resolution of the conflict in central and eastern Europe and in the Middle East took longer. The Austro-Hungarian and Ottoman states had collapsed, and their empires were divided up in a number of different treaties. There was more fighting, such as between Greece and the new state of Turkey.

KEY DATES

November 11, 1918 Armistice on the Western Front. German armies have been defeated and return to Germany.

January-June, 1919 Discussions between the Allied leaders in the Paris Peace Conference lead to the Versailles Treaty being signed in June. Germany agrees to pay huge reparations and admit its guilt for the war.

September 1919 The collapse of the Austro-Hungarian Empire and its dissolution into a number of successor states in the Treaty of Saint-Germain-en-Laye.

June 1920 Treaty of Trianon. Hungary, which had severed its links with Austria, makes peace with the Allies and is reduced in size.

August 1920 Treaty of Sevres between the Ottoman Empire and the Allies. The Empire is broken up and its Middle East possessions (Lebanon, Syria, Iraq, and Palestine, for example) become "Mandates" ruled by Western powers.

July 1923 Turkey refuses to accept the Treaty of Sevres. After heavy fighting, Treaty of Lausanne replaces the Treaty of Sevres, creating the state of Turkey.

1 The signing of the Versailles Treaty in June 1919. Woodrow Wilson is at center, holding a copy of the document.

2 The punitive reparations imposed on Germany were opposed by many at the time, who saw them as setting up future problems.

3 The French, British, and Italian premiers (the central three seated figures) insisted upon Germany accepting its guilt for the war.

4 Greek troops move into Smyrna, now Izmir, in what is now Turkey. The Greek population of the city was forced out in 1923 after the war between Greece and Turkey.

Glossary

armistice A halt in fighting agreed to by both sides.

artillery Weapons for discharging missiles.

assassination A murder by sudden or secret attack, often for political reasons.

blockade The isolation by a warring nation of an enemy area to prevent the passage of people or supplies.

bombard To attack with artillery.

casualty A military person lost through death, injury, sickness, or capture.

cruiser A fast, heavily armed warship.

deadlock A situation in which nothing changes.

division A military unit of between 10,000 and 20,000 troops.

dogfight A battle between two or more fighter planes.

expeditionary force Part of an army sent to fight in a foreign country.

flank The right or left wing of an army.

howitzer A type of field gun.

infantry Soldiers trained, armed, and equipped to fight on foot.

merchant ship A civilian vessel that carries cargo or passengers.

morale The emotional and spiritual strength of a person or people.

no-man's land An unoccupied area of land between two opposing armies.

offensive A group of military attacks.

rations Shares of food or provisions determined by supply.

salient A part of a front line that projects into enemy territory.

sector A section of a military front line.

stalemate A deadlocked position between opposing sides.

tank A tracked armored fighting vehicle.

terrain The physical features of an area of land.

trench A long cut in the ground that serves as a military defense.

ultimatum A final demand which, if not met, will lead to war.

uprising A violent rebellion against a government.

zeppelin A long, thin, motor-powered airship.

Further Resources

Books

Bearce, Stephanie. *Spies, Secret Missions, and Hidden Facts from World War I.* Routledge, 2021.

Ford, Jeanne Marie. *The Role of Women in World War I.* The Child's World, 2018.

Hunter, Nick. *World War I: Frontline Soldiers and Their Families.* Rosen Publishing, 2017.

Knutson, Julie. *World War I: The Great War to End All Wars.* Nomad Press, 2022.

Meadows, William C. *The First Code Talkers: Native American Communicators in World War I.* University of Oklahoma Press, 2021.

Neiberg, Michael S. *World War I Illustrated Atlas.* Amber Books, 2022.

Nelson, Kristen Rajczak. *World War I.* Cavendish Square, 2022.

Smithsonian Museum. *World War I, the Definitive Visual History.* Dorling Kindersley, 2018.

Wilkins, Mark C. *German Fighter Aircraft in World War I.* Casemate Illustrated, 2021.

Websites

www.firstworldwar.com
A multimedia history of World War I.

www.bbc.co.uk/history/worldwars/wwone
BBC site about the war, including movies and audio galleries.

spartacus-educational.com/FWW.htm
Spartacus Educational index to World War I for students.

www.pbs.org/wgbh/americanexperience/films/great-war/
PBS Internet companion to *The Great War.*

www.eyewitnesstohistory.com/w1frm.htm
Dozens of eyewitness accounts from the conflict.

www.theworldwar.org/interactive-wwi-timeline
An interactive timeline.

Index